Joy: The Five Lights that Clarify Your Best Self Through the Pain

By Samantina Zenon

First Edition: May 2021

Joy: The Five Lights that Clarify Your Best Self Through the Pain/ By Samantina Zenon

ISBN: **978-1-943616-39-8**

Publisher: MAWMedia Group, LLC
Los Angeles | Reno | Nashville

Table of Contents

Preface: My Story, Your Lights

This is an inspirational book that teaches You about resilience and creating the person you want to be. My story is a story of triumph. I want to show where I started and where I am now. There is no limit if you take control of your life. Heal yourself from your trauma. You can be your best self. The process of healing is painful. Trauma is a scar that you carry all your life. You must not let that scar define you. Refuse to let that be the end of your story.

My definition of me: I am a daring dreamer who took action to make my dreams happen. The rejection of life could not stop me. I felt like giving up at times, but I was motivated by not wanting to waste my time. I don't always feel my best. I take a break, and I keep going.

Some situations remind me of what happened, and my negative thoughts challenge me. If this is a similar experience for you, speak to yourself with affirmations. I speak to my challenge of comparing myself to others. "You have come a long way. You have accomplished a lot that you do not give yourself credit for. You must focus on the next level." I practice encouraging myself to continue toward what I want for my life. I make a list of my accomplishments. I refocus on the truth of my bright future.

I am motivated, happy, and fueled for the next activity. I know that my hard work will not go unnoticed. My mornings begin extremely early because I am putting in the work to build the future that I want. My concern is not to repeat the same cycles as I have experienced growing up. I want to hold myself accountable for my choices.

I had not realized how much I was carrying an unconscious burden. You just think that the world is messed up. That's true. But the people you allow within the circle are your choice. The person you lay down with at night is a choice you make and must live with or change.

I want new parents and future parents to ask themselves this question:

What are three things you wish you received as a child from your parents?

Whatever your list of three are, pour them into your children just as you would want them for yourself! My list includes love, protection, and emotional support. I want to provide these, instill them as reality, and pass them down as abilities to my future kids. Write yours down as a reminder. I simply cannot imagine my children feeling the way I felt as a child.

Section I: My Origin

Chapter 1: Preparing for the Moment

My mom was the girl in her family growing up. She says she was more like a maid to them growing up. I have tried to talk to her about my upbringing. She makes only excuses. Her need for validation created scars for me both literally and figuratively. I had to heal internally as well as externally.

My Mother

My mom was physically, emotionally, psychologically abusive. I could never make mistakes. I internalized her requirements and felt I must do everything right the first time, even without training. She exacted perfection. When it was not achieved, her punishments were brutal.

When I was growing up in Haiti, she would send me to the store as a test. She had a weird practice of spitting on the floor. "If this spit dries out, that means you took too long." I don't remember ever arriving home before the spit dried. She would beat me without concern for how long the checkout line was or any difficulties I overcame in the process. Seemingly, her only purpose was to punish me.

I remember once, she was yelling at me for something minor. I didn't want her to hit me and began to flinch, stepping backwards. She was boiling beans on a hot plate on the floor. I kicked it by accident as she watched, and I burned my feet. Afterward, she hit me with an electrical cord, which created a scar on my right breast to this day. She was a predator to her own child.

My older sister's experience was the same. They do not get along. My mum believes she is our mother and can do whatever she wants. They constantly fight, both verbally and physically, whenever they are under the same roof. Or, should I say my mother is violent toward my sister. She pulls knives, calls names, and perpetuates all manners of violence.

The challenge for my sister is that she is dependent upon my mother. My sister doesn't choose the best men. She is repeating the cycle of seeking validation in her life. Unlike me, she did not get away to college after graduating high school. My uncle convinced my mother not to allow her to go away for college. He said that my sister would turn to drugs and return broken. My sister blames my mother for all her bad choices while dismissing herself or taking responsibility for her actions.

My mother does not think that anything is wrong with her. She deflects everything. She signed up for parent loans for me to attend college. She holds that over my head, although I am the one repaying them. She believes that this was her greatest achievement. She wanted me to graduate college just so that she could brag about it. She is duplicitous and deceptive, always attempting to paint herself in a favorable light. She seems to do this often with people that are not impressed or could not be bothered with her—a recipe for failure and disappointment.

She told her sisters that I forged her signature on the parent-student loan. I was not able to pay the loan right away. My mother used this as a weapon against me. Her version was that I took a loan, did not tell her about it, and now, she must pay the loan. Her sisters believed her. One suggested that she should report me to the police as a perpetrator of fraud and sue me. The true story is that she did not have enough income to secure the loan herself. We both went to her father to ask him to cosign for the loan. He agreed. Her complaints of forgery and fraud are baseless. She knows this. But she perpetuates the lie for the benefit of validation from her sisters. On one hand, she takes pride in the fact that I completed my college education. On the other hand, she promotes the idea that I committed fraud to obtain the school loan.

She continues to make decisions based on people who do not mean her well. She wants people to know that she has a daughter that will stick up for her. She had a job where her bosses were abusive. I had to go to the job and inform them that we will not tolerate abuse and would pursue any mistreatment with the proper authorities. I found out that my mother volunteered to go to the supervisor's house to clean it. Though she made it clear that she was mistreated at the workplace, she chose to go to the supervisor's house. She does these things for validation. She thought she would gain from going the extra mile. She wants to be perceived as a good person. She often does what she thinks will give her clout. It rarely turns out that way.

If I attempt to tell her when people are using her or when a situation is not healthy, she will go off. She will even hit me in defense of her choices. Usually, less than a month later, she will come back to me asking me to defend her from the person or to fix the situation she had found herself mistreated in.

My Father
Basically, my father was an alcoholic. He was also jealous. People must have told him that they saw my mom with another guy or that she was

cheating. I don't know where he got intoxicated, but he would come home at 3:00 in the morning to fight my mom. My mom felt like her children were part of the problem. She would often tell us that she never loved him. It seemed that she connected with him out of convenience. It was hurtful to hear that she only stayed with him because of us. I often felt like a burden. He never abused or mistreated us.

One night, he came home drunk. My maternal grandmother had passed. My mom moved in with one of her brothers from her father's side. You could hear the thunder crashing outside. My uncle came down and told him that he needed to leave. My father argued with my uncle until my uncle went to get a machete. My uncle forbade him from coming back. He was around and always a part of our lives though he was no longer in the home. We spent time with him at his family home. We also spent time with him at his home.

He was a product of a home that created an intense need for love. He was one of eleven kids. He was dark-skinned in a country that favored fair-skinned people. He connected with a woman who could not provide that love. They were never married. He did not live with us but would come over, stay a couple of days, then leave. He wanted her love because she was fair-skinned and attractive by all standards. I believe the alcohol was a way to numb his pain.

I remember I was getting my hair done by a woman for my first communion. The woman said to another woman at the beauty salon, "What is a beautiful woman like that doing with an ugly man like that?" In the Haitian culture, men and woman bleach their skin, thinking that lighter, fairer skin is more beautiful. My father doesn't like talking about the past, but I know that the pressure of the culture and his upbringing weighed on him.

I used to feel bad for my mom. She was mistreated because of what he heard. He returned late at night. They were involved in physical fights. As children, we were awakened and watched the violence unfold. This led to me not feeling safe. That night, when my father left, he was injured by a plate thrown by my mother. He limped for weeks because the cut was so deep.

Mom next met a jeweler. He was light-skinned and attractive. He was also promiscuous, disrespectful, and abusive. Unlike her relationship with my father, my mother never fought back. The abuse was so intense that my sister and I got involved once. She loved him and did not want him to leave her. It was like she was head over heels. I remember, once, she was sitting on her bed crying her eyes out after a fight where he beat the crap out of her. Her best friend was there attempting to console her. "I love him so much. I don't know what to do."

Lessons from My Past

People often think that the woman is the only one who suffers in a domestic violence situation. The children suffer too. Studies have reported that children from violent homes will repeat that cycle. The reality is that a home filled with alcoholism, insecurity, and abuse becomes normal. The triggers are comfortable. When relationships form, what should be seen as red flags are seen as attractive because they are comfortable.

Abuse must not be repeated. I have identified alcohol as a major red flag in relationships. A person that turns to alcohol or drugs as a way to make themselves feel better is not a healthy person. You must get the help you need to deal with the trauma and work through it. Seek a counselor that can help you walk through it and discover techniques to counteract your post-traumatic stress. Toxic relationships have a way of perpetuating themselves. People in these relationships fear abandonment. Even though pain is a part of the experience, they see the interactions as their partner's love language. They stay because they do not want to be alone.

Another lesson is to love yourself first. When you come across people in your life, you must know how to discern between love, lust, and obsession. Beating you is not based on love. Controlling you is not based on love. Loving yourself peals away the blinders on relationships. You may have been trained that your parents spank you because they love you. I see so many examples on social media of parents who are praised for acting violently towards their children, including cursing, hitting, and other abuse. Our society does not portray healthy communication, kindness, and consistency to reach people and change hearts and minds. We hold violence as a tool for change. It seems cliché, but you must give love a chance to work. Begin with loving yourself. Refuse to waste your time with a person that keeps you trapped in your past.

Chapter 2: Cycles

Defining a Woman

What I lost in my childhood is the bond with my mother. I learned how to be a woman by myself. I did not make all the right decisions. I also did not know when I was doing the right thing. I walked on eggshells without training or guidance. I did not find a solid direction until later in life.

My mother was not a woman to us. She was really young when she had us. Mothers are supposed to be nurturing, but everyone does not have a nurturing mom. There were times I would daydream about having a mom that was like those on social media enjoying life with their children. I truly don't know how my life would be different. Your mom should be a role model for you. That is the way it should be. Lack of a solid and healthy bond can wreak havoc on a child and set a young adult up for failure.

I wrote an article discussing the reality of #GirlDad. A girl cannot learn to be a woman from a man. A man is a man. A man can't teach a woman about puberty and menstruation. He does not understand female emotions and sensitivities. These are jobs for a mother. A mother is critical to the development of daughters, just as fathers are critical to sons' development.

I felt like a woman was the weaker sex. My mother showed an example of someone who accepted abuse and disrespect. I was taught to stay in my lane and not rub people the wrong way. I now know that being a woman is ensuring, advocating, and loving your voice. A woman is not a weaker vessel. She is strong, not in the cliché sense, but in the sense that she is equal to any task. She is proud, passionate, and persistent in the areas she knows are right, just, and progressive.

Describing a Cycle

I want to be a better parent to children than I may have. The point is to break the cycle. My mom had a poor relationship with her mom but raised us the same way. She did not realize that she was like her mom in many ways. She is a follower. She listens to advice from others even when it is wrong and ill-informed. She also seems oblivious to both her failure to provide a loving, supportive home and the sheer force of will it took for me to succeed at anything.

I signed up for a pageant in high school. I had to fundraise for everything. My mother did not give a dollar for the fees. In addition, I had to beg her to come and support me. I had to sneak and obtain her bank account to deposit money from sponsorships. When the time came to pay the hotel fees, she checked her bank account and bragged that she had the money to help me. But before paying, she regaled us of visions of spending her newfound wealth on a lavish lifestyle. She took that moment, made it about her, and stressed me out.

I put money in her account to pay for the hotel. I thought the hotel would take the money from the account without my mother's intervention. I did not know how hotels worked. My mother tried to act like all the money was hers. Not only did she not want to pay for the fees, but she also wanted to use the money for herself. Thank goodness I had told my sister about the fundraising. She backed me up, and my mother paid for the hotel fees with her bankcard.

I was afraid that I worked hard for something and she was going to take it away. The experience reinforced my anxiety because I had to beg from her. She told me she could not help. I looked for sponsors, raised the money, and she wanted to take it from me. I made the reservations for the hotel. They told me I was all set. The challenge began when we arrived at the hotel check-in. I felt like I was in trouble for something that was not my fault. It was another thing that I did not do right.

When I graduated, I knew I was going to get away from the household and my mother's abuse. I understood that people must mature and seek their own way as they grow older. But I was also shacked by always trying to do the right thing. I felt like I was walking on eggshells. I was trying to be perfect all the time, but I was making mistakes. Those mistakes felt like the end of the world.

You're Fired

I was a resident assistant. I was fired. That's the short version of the story. The full version is clear after reflection. I was bullied by students who were constantly throwing parties. In my official duties, I was often called by complaining students to shut the parties down. The volleyball team and basketball teams were the consistent culprits. I felt that these students were disturbing students who took their education seriously. I was sure that any administrators would back me up on this.

I wrote incident reports and submitted them. The students would tell me all the time that the reports would not make a difference. They taunted me. I shared a suite with another RA who was like a mentor, having been on the job longer than I had. I asked her for advice on what to do, informing her that I was considering contacting the coaches of the student-athletes. She agreed that I send an email. I emailed the coaches. "Please address your athletes. They continue to receive Incident Reports related to their disruptive behavior in the dorms." I thought that if I spoke up, the coaches would support the education of the students that were being disruptive. I thought that going the extra mile beyond incident reports would have a positive result. I thought sending the email would bring some resolution. I was naïve. The volleyball coach was the only coach to respond. He sent so many emails—to everyone, from my supervisor to the provost. He also sent me a nasty email telling me not to email him.

My boss had to go to several meetings. He was extremely angry with me. I was disturbed and disappointed. Prior to this, I worked overtime fulfilling my duties as an RA. I would stay up all night attempting to make things right. I had security telling me that I was the best RA. I followed up. I was responsive and attentive. I went from being RA of the week one week to being fired the next.

The lesson that I took right away was not to go the extra mile. I felt like I was set up. I do not want to blame the mentor who told me to move forward. I felt like my supervisor had an issue with me from the beginning. He seemed to taunt me purposefully. I had to move out of the RA suite. He put me into a room with two nasty individuals. They were so horrible that I had to move out. I did not know why this person had so much animosity toward me.

The greater revelation came soon after. I knew that this supervisor was intimidating, if not overbearing. I chose to sign up to be under him anyway. I recognized something attractive. I was a leader on campus. I was focused on developing my leadership abilities and living in the dorm for free. It would take me some time in therapy to realize the connection to my mother. It would take me longer to unpack this and become conscious enough to make decisions that are in my best interest.

I still work on analyzing situations, asking the right questions, and accepting that people do not give you all the details at the start of interactions, relationships, or employment. I am working on using my best judgment. I also ask for help and communicate with people that I judge to be supportive. I make decisions to be around people that are good for me.

I now look for the red flags in relationships, but it is important for me to have a sense of self that is independent of others. My validation will not be sought from others. I must develop it from within. I look for real connections with people beyond the transactional nature of the world. Unfortunately, most people portray a persona of grace and achievement. They deny the truth of trauma they experienced in childhood. They think it is too hard to work on. If you want to create the best version of yourself, you must deconstruct yourself like broken pieces of glass. People who are not about that life typically fall away quickly.

Chapter 3: Making Mistakes

In response to being fired and the aftermath in college, I sought counseling. Therapy was the beginning of my ability to fire everyone from the position of validation for my life. Validation comes from within. I know who I am. No one can take my truth, autonomy, or identity from me. Searching for validation will only disappoint you. To be self-validated is the foundation of self-advocacy. People and situations will try you. Self-advocacy enables you to resist, reframe, and recover when needed.

Therapy

I had to see a therapist in college. I walked into the office and immediately recognized the noise-cancelling device they used. I cannot describe the sound, but it kept the conversation confidential. I had built a wall. I did not address anything in my life emotionally. My therapist would ask me to open up. My throat would get extremely tight and hurtful. I could not respond. It was a territory that I was not able to tread upon.

It took me six months of anxiety taking over my body before I had a breakthrough. The tears would not flow for six months. My anxieties came from my childhood upbringing to always be perfect. I remember I sang a song by Nina Simone, 4 Woman. I had not allowed the words to connect with me even though I learned the song. In the song, she speaks about four types of Black women. She literally sings about racism and slavery, but I interpreted it differently. The day I broke down was the day after the jazz recital.

My mom was a slave to the way that she lived her life. She was a mental slave to her culture. I reflected on that in connection with the lyrics to the song and broke down. I finally cried in the session for the first time ever. I sat there crying for the whole session. Normally, the therapist would ask how my week had gone. We would talk about incidents and how I could have handled them differently. I told her about my recital. I told her about the song I sang. I told her that the song was recommended by a friend. She asked that we talk about the lyrics. She was a white woman. I don't know if she knew the song or the lyrics. At that moment, I lost it.

As I cried, she asked questions seeking to support my breakthrough. I got through the session. From that session, my sessions included my emotions. I cried in every other session after that. I was able to see the trauma I had been through and my approach to managing it. I had learned to be numb and emotionless. I buried my emotions and did not feel them consciously.

I did not see how my childhood trauma impacted my adulthood. I was carrying the burdens of childhood. "Do you see that you had a mother who would not allow you to make mistakes, and your director fired you for one mistake." This was my wakeup call and the beginning of my healing. The work from there was to discover a new way to live my life. It was an intentional effort not to repeat the same relationships and practices. Emotionally, the hurt was presented as something to deconstruct, reframe, and integrate.

I saw that therapist for three years. In each session, we unpacked so much. I realized that this woman didn't love me. I thought always keeping it together, not crying, getting over it, was a part of me. I thought I had to know what to do in every situation, even without being taught. I grew up thinking that the situation was me against the world.

I would always blame myself if things did not go right. From my mother to my boss to early boyfriends, I took the blame even when I should not. In therapy, I learned to allow myself to make mistakes and learn from my experience. I also learned to see the situation and separate my choices from others' choices. I can accept my accountability and allow them to handle theirs. I can be kind to myself and consider grace even while learning and improving where possible.

Stay in Your Lane

When I told my mom, she showed no sympathy. "Why didn't you stay in your lane?" She always has a way to make me feel guilty about something. She would tell me to stay in my lane, but she stayed in her lane at her job and was still treated badly. She failed to learn the lesson of her experience. The weird thing is that people perpetuate this with comments like, "Be careful." Being careful in situations where you feel unsafe is ridiculous. The "careful" they are speaking of will have you ill-prepared, unresponsive, and targeted by abuse.

Instead, you must stand up and take action if you believe that you can make a difference. You cannot stay in your lane and allow people to abuse you. When your identity and right to exist is being threatened, there is no staying in your lane. You must do something to address the threat.

You must be in tune with yourself and pay close attention to what you are triggered by. Being in tune with yourself begins with accepting reality. I attempted to cover up my history with my mother with a blanket of, "It is my mother. It is all good. She did the best she could." I did not give her the responsibility for her toxic behavior initially. I internalized that pain. I was raised around negativity and did not see a different way.

There can be a light at the end of the tunnel if you create that light. It will take work, but you must be committed to putting in that work. You will feel low when you see others advancing if you are not making the choice to develop and mature. We live in a society where you are trained to pretend and seek the quick fix. Working toward your best is seeking enduring happiness with yourself. Seeking a good space, facing challenges, working through trauma is a healthy lifestyle. Blaming others, self-medicating for the outside, and ignoring the inside are signs of poor mental health. If you have experienced trauma, accept that the work will continue throughout your life.

I have found joy in the process. I used to feel defeat when I was rejected. You are not going to be accepted by everyone in your life. Relationships are supposed to be reciprocal. Find those relationships that are beneficial to you and the other person.

Narcissists Do Nothing Wrong

My mother continues in attempts to shame me for being independent, talking poorly about me. I limit contact. I know the feeling of guilt that comes from that choice. I was raised around the idea that you must honor your parents. It doesn't matter if the person makes you feel unsafe. People believe that you should engage with your parents regardless of their behavior. "It's your mom. The negatives don't matter." I remember that response from a person after I shared my story. How dare you tell anyone that their safety is not important! You must seek your health, safety, and security as a priority. You cannot justify the violence and abuse of any vulnerable person. Your parents do not get a pass on righteous and healthy behavior.

I told my mother about what she did as a parent. She responded, "Every parent does that, curse their child and calls them bad names." She is self-absorbed. She can do no wrong. She does not care about my emotions.

People often allow their ego to get the best of them. Rather than apologies, they go on social media and write out arguments and spew venom. It all stems from how they were raised. They never learned conflict resolution. Rather than address the problem like an adult, they take the social media route toward pettiness and immaturity.

I have recognized the narcissistic fallacy that anything goes as long as everyone is doing it. Since I have been on this journey, I have found that it is harder to make friends. Too many people live their lives with unresolved hurt. It is not entertaining to do the physical, mental, and emotional work to heal from past trauma.

Social media is a part of my life because of the work I do. But social media is not for going back and forth in arguments. I have caught myself commenting on posts and responding to the lives of celebrities. I had to realize how easily I was influenced to engage in petty behavior. I stopped following certain pages because they did not add value to my life.

You must reflect on the value your activities, experiences, and choices bring to your life. It cannot be entertainment only. The experiences you consume impact you in some way, whether positive or negative. I remember seeing a woman confronting a reality tv star in an airport. People often say that reality television is entertaining. "It's not to be taken seriously," they say. But the fact that you have feelings about it tells you that it has some impact. When you watch films, you laugh, cry, or have some reaction to them. Understand that your hormones and endorphins are triggered by what is consumed in your environment.

Chapter 4: Therapy Pitch

The Challenge Ahead

You have been through a lot. Seek therapy to understand and process the pain. Obviously, it will be challenging to address the issues. You must go through the pain to experience the joy.

The stigma around mental health is disappointing. It is terrible that people walk around needing to be better and heal from trauma without knowing how or allowing themselves to seek therapy. I remember talking to a pastor and offering therapy resources. "My parishioners may use it, but I don't need it." Really? This pastor thought that because he gave out advice, he was both qualified as a counselor and not in need of counseling. I could not resist asking him whether he had studied human behavior. He admitted that he had not. But he insisted that he was able to guide people in their physical, mental, and emotional lives in addition to their spiritual practices. Of course, this is a common fallacy.

Many people with anxiety do not think they are diagnosable. That was my belief too. I did not know that the upset in my belly, the tightness in my throat, and the dissatisfaction in my life was anxiety. I did not make the connection until I began to see a therapist.

I remember going live on Instagram on Mental Health Day to talk about anxiety. I described the symptoms of anxiety. A girl chimed in with an epiphany. "This is what anxiety is? I feel like this all the time when I am under pressure or stressed." I explained where my anxiety came from and how I engaged in therapy. I do not know what the woman did with the information, but I hope she persisted. I also engaged with others who supported the idea of therapy from personal experience.

The challenge is to expand your definition of self-care. Self-care is not only physical. It is emotional and mental. Looking good on the outside and feeling bad on the inside is not acceptable. You need to take care of Yourself as a whole. You must learn to see things for what they truly are. You do not need to confront the people who have hurt you. You do not need to convince them that they were wrong. You CAN move forward and attract people who support your best self and influence greater outcomes in your life. It is a hard task, but it is worth it. NO one will invest in you the way you will invest in yourself.

Pessimist

I expected the worst in situations. I experienced anxiety to the point where I would puke whenever something went wrong. I had not made the connection between my upbringing and my health. It took me a long time to realize that things will work out in the end. It sounds simple, but it was not so simple for me.

My pessimism kept me from enjoying the experience. For example, when I sang for recitals, I was motivated to get it over with. I was putting in the work to get results, but I was not in a healthy space. I was controlled by the anxiety. People would tell me that I did a good job, but I was always focused on the negatives and the mistakes. I did not want to believe their words of comparison. After performing, I would sit in the bathroom, comparing myself to other singers. I thought they were good, and I was not.

I still feel scared when it is time to perform. I talk myself out of negative thoughts. I train to switch from pessimism to optimism. I know that my focus will result in success. I cannot fail, but if I do, I will pick myself up and continue forward. Things do not always work out as planned. I can contribute to the situation. I can change my environment. I can do my best always. Giving up is an option as long as I don't give up on myself. I can walk away from situations that do not suit me or that I don't feel supported in, and I can give myself grace.

For me, it is good versus evil. You attempt to think positive, but negative is what you have practiced. I felt the need to control everything. That inclination comes from insecurity—part of feeling that is born in desiring to be safe. Safety and security are primal and basic needs. I was used to walking on a straight line—to be perfect on that line. It is a daily allowance of grace to accept that I can veer from that line and still be worthy of safety and security.

Power of The Connection

Anxiety results from the feeling of someone else calling the shots. When you process your pain and make the connections, you take your power back, which enables you to heal. People cannot use something against you when you have addressed it. You can experience healing resulting from your intentional choice to work through your trauma.

I feel I had to learn everything over again. It was almost like I was reborn. I seek to live life with purpose and intentionality. I will not allow people to abuse me. I make sure I am around people that respect me. I will train people how to treat me by managing my relationships and my environment. I had to learn not to allow people to disrespect me.

You recognize a cycle the moment you connect your past trauma and your present choices. I knew my boss was stern and intimidating, but I did not realize that he was like my mother. I still went after the job. I did not know my mental health, triggers, and how that connected to me feeling bad about myself. I was optimistic to the point of being naïve. I did not know to be conscious and guard my mental health.

Every opportunity will not be a good experience for you. I am not saying that you must refuse and be guarded to the point of refusing all opportunities. Don't give up if things get hard but recognize the red flags that surface initially. Manage your mental health. Respond to your triggers rather than reacting. Make and sustain your peace.

That need for validation will cause you to feel that you must prove yourself. You feel that you must prove that you are good enough. I see articles about burnout all the time. The best way to avoid burnout is to know your limitations. Also, know that you are enough—good enough, smart enough, capable enough. I had to write the things that I am proud of that I can use to remind myself of my progress.

You must give yourself time to care for yourself. Take time to celebrate the small wins, including simple acts of taking care of yourself. Accept the connection between your past trauma and your current choices. Redress your past trauma as an origin. Review your current choices through a lens of possibilities. You are worthy no matter if you were cheered on as a child or damaged and abused. Learn to believe that you are good enough.

Section II: From Pain to Joy

Chapter 5: Set Boundaries

You must work on yourself and get into a place where you are not selling yourself short. You must reach a point where you are accountable for Yourself. Create an environment that supports your goals.

If you don't set boundaries, you will be played. Users will come and take and take until you are dry. They do not care about your feelings or your security.

People seem to be clueless about genuine relationships. You can't just text someone on social media and ask for money to buy something. They don't even greet or say hello. They don't think of the process of relating to another person. That is the normal interaction with people today. Users take that to another level. They are in your face when you can provide something for them. When you cannot, they are on to the next.

People with boundaries and those who accept boundaries understand that no one owes you anything. Expectations of anything from anyone is set up for disappointment. Users feel entitled for whatever reason.

I have experienced challenges in creating genuine relationships because people are traumatized by users. I am big on meeting people. I enjoyed having pen pals back before social media. I have connected with people overseas and visited subsequently and had a great time. It is not about using people.

The beginning of a boundary is creating genuine relationships. People who are genuine take the time to build genuine rapport. They connect on multiple levels. Users have a typical set of ideals in stark contrast to authentic individuals.

Entitlement. The key distinction between a genuine person and a user is the sense of entitlement of the user. For example, if you have $10, they will ask you for the $10 and not worry about what you have left.

False Benefit. Users pretend that they are benefitting you while they are attempting to use you. They set up scenarios so that they can get what they want out of it.

Inconsistency. Another indicator of users is that they only come around when they need something. They will make a contribution of time until they get what they want. Once they get what they want, they are gone until the next time they need something.

Anger Issues. The final indicator is when you don't give in to their desires, they get angry. I remember a person I thought was a friend who refused to give me a promised ride because I refused to split a bill evenly. I paid for what I consumed.

Slander. When you don't allow a user to use you, they will make up stories that support the idea that you are inconsiderate. They spend time to set you up by lying about who you are over time to anyone who cares to listen, like in that situation at the restaurant with girls that I thought were friends. They went on to spread the lie that I was inconsiderate because I did not allow them to use me.

Your Change toward Self-Respect

Toxic people will begin to think you are attempting to be better than them. People who do not understand what you are doing and how you are changing can be removed from your life. I cut off those so-called friends who violated my boundaries and showed themselves to be users.

There were two of them that were the greatest challenges. One was the instigator that sought to gaslight me into a reaction. I refused. When she attempted to tell me I was overreacting in the restaurant, I shut her down with calm tones and called an Uber. When she went on social media and spoke ill of me, I did not react. I refused to add fire. I refused to be set up even though she worked hard to put me in a spot.

The other was the one who was supposed to give me a ride. I called for Uber and left. She followed up later, attempting to be nice. "You didn't even say goodbye to me." She wanted to clean up the interaction and assess whether we were still good.

"No hard feelings." I kept it moving. If she chose to follow her friend and deny me something promised. If you are so easily influenced, if you leave me in a bind on a whim, you are not genuine to me. You were never my friend in the first place.

I have realized that people respond to negativity. They seek attention. I don't know whether it is because of their trauma, miseducation, or whatever the reason may be, but people seem okay with pretending.

P a g e |43

I am not. I will not plot against someone because of the pretense that I created that I am for you. I refuse to be that invested.

Give your energy to things that build you. This is the basis of self-respect. Going back and forth with someone on social media is immature. Attempting to be polite with someone you do not like or respect is wasted energy. Drama sells. Some people think that drama is an acceptable way to live their lives. It is not. Drama and stress are why heart disease is the number one killer in the United States.

Once you begin to set boundaries for yourself, you will lose people you thought were friends. Quality is better than quantity when it comes to friends. I do not need "friends" that bring out negatives in me. I do not need people in my circle that stress me, require perfection, and promote drama and toxicity.

Limiting Exposure

You may need to reduce contact with some people to simple check-ins. When you release these people, you gain clarity. Your productivity increases tremendously.

Arguments change your mode. It causes a definite change in energy. This is a critical element of mental health. Your trauma can be triggered through unhealthy interactions. Your energy switches to address the trigger rather than building whatever could have been built for your progress and productivity.

When you have positive energy around you, the clarity comes from a **better sense of yourself**. It gives you purpose and the desire to do more. For example, when you are happy with your job, you are motivated to get there and produce. Sitting with supportive people in a healthy environment is a wonderful way to live. You make better choices in what you eat, what you spend your time doing, and how you maintain your health. You refuse to self-medicate with temporary fixes.

Repeating Patterns

I remember a person who I was dating even after my therapy. We were dating a week when we attended a Thanksgiving party. His friend's baby dad's stepfather attempted to warn me about the situation. He told me about his drinking problem. The friend who invited him to the party noticed that I was telling him to stop drinking. She said, "Why did you keep bringing these bougie women around where you can't be yourself?" He went to the bathroom to keep drinking. He followed me as I left.

I video recorded him drunk out of his mind. I confronted him the next day. He explained and apologized. It got worse. He would come over to my place drunk. He would always want to go to bars. He would pick fights about petty things. I began to notice a pattern.

I said to myself, "How can I leave this relationship? I am not going to repeat the situation I endured in my childhood." I was convinced that I would end it and never come back. But I came back. I also reflect now on the needs that I had for companionship. Maybe no one ever confronted him and helped him through his alcoholism. In my mind, I could help. That also makes me a good person. I recognize now that my need was to control the situation. This is never a recipe for success. You cannot change another person. They must be willing to change themselves.

We broke up two times before I finally ended it for good. After we broke up, he would lie and say that he was going to a therapist. He would say that he changed and was drinking less. He even told me that his mother died. He did not change. He justified his behavior by saying that "Every normal man drink five or more bottles of beers daily after work."

He would come home arguing. I realized that I had to end the relationship because he was repeating a pattern. Toxic relationships will have you thinking that they are improving. The lies and deceit in a toxic relationship are juxtaposed against the positives in the relationship. Maybe the sex is good, or the financial support is encouraging. But the relationship is toxic. It causes undue stress and exacerbates anxiety.

He also attempted to tell me that no one else would love me like he does. That sounded sweet initially, but I recognized it as his need for control by the end. He wanted to point out my flaws, belittle me, and use that to justify his toxic choices. No amount of good will overcome toxicity. He seemed to play on my needs and the information about myself that I gave him. My need fed his dysfunction. It took me a while to stop myself from compromising in the toxicity—to see the compliments for what they were. I was enabling him to treat me badly. He gave me the attention I needed at the moment. He was funny and engaging. The challenge was that I saw the red flags in that first situation at the party. I disregarded the flags and immediately launched into "I can help mode." When he was able to explain, I was committed.

A healthy relationship does not have friction that threatens your mental health. The truth of the matter is that healthy relationships are out there. You will not see them if you are in a horrible relationship. Make a list of what you will accept and what you will not.

My end to the relationship was setting a boundary for a healthy relationship. I chose to prioritize myself and move on. I was not going to lower myself to his level. I was not going to embrace the challenge of stress, arguing, and alcoholism for the sake of being in a relationship. I understood that I could not fix this man. I understood that this is not my responsibility. I must bring health to a relationship. Hopefully, the other person brings health as well.

I had to set a boundary. I looked at the relationship and its outcomes five years down the road. I knew that my need for companionship could not be allowed to destroy my peace. The good times could not excuse the fighting. I had to choose that this was unacceptable.

Take the time after these experiences to reflect on your experiences. Apply the lessons to your personal life and your relationships. Become what you want to accept. Own you and who you are. When you do, people cannot come to you with nonsense. Observe people with the understanding that you can judge what is best for yourself. Fast forward to one date with a person who drank like a fish. I never went out with him again. Good for me!

Chapter 6: Persist in Therapy

We make parents out to be heroes. We seem to want to push our feelings under the rug. We don't want to deal with our traumas. We act in such a way that if something doesn't happen to us; we can't relate. At least, that is the reality of social media. Many of us are a product of parents who are horrible to their kids. Where I'm from in Haiti, kids are on the street because their parents don't give a damn about them. Little boys who are thrown into the streets grow up to kidnap people just to make making and take care of their needs. What did we think was going to happen? No one talks about that full story. No one seems to demonstrate a desire to address the issues. We want to portray the "happy family," but then we show reality television and expose the ills of families.

Suicidal Ideation

I would cry my heart out every time I went through therapy. I would be defeated by the idea that my mom did not love me. The first time she said I love you, I was 22 years old. I did not know how to respond. I think she may have heard it from a friend talking to their children. I did not feel that she felt it authentically.

Healing requires solitude but not isolation. You must get away from toxic people, but you must seek out supportive people and environments. You will not get results without supportive people around you. You will have stones thrown for stepping out of the box of social norms. Ninety percent of people are not ready to have children. The problem is that they do not seem to be in a hurry to get the healing that prepares them to support the health of children. I often hear people say, "No one is ever ready to be a parent." I think that is a poor excuse for people who choose to be irresponsible. Ultimately, being a parent is a choice. You are the first role model your child will meet. Make the meeting worthwhile.

I see how that decision impacts the family. Potential parents must consider the required tasks of checking in with children no matter what else is going on in life. Work, leisure, chores, and emergencies are facts of life. But a parent must be available for parenting. That is if we want the best results.

It is not rocket science to check in with your kids. It does not require advanced ability to give quality time to a child. Many parents think that providing material things is their only responsibility. I remember I worked in Bloomingdales observing children of 11 years old coming in with their black cards. Their parents were absent in business meetings or other activities. They sent the kids into the store for retail therapy. Cognitive Behavioral therapy will eventually be needed. But the simplest solution is to parent.

One of my aunts died by suicide. We were told that it was because she could not be with the man she loved. She fell into depression when he was in the Army. That never made sense to me. There must be more to it. My maternal grandfather had 13 children by multiple women. My aunt was looking for love that she never received in the family. Her fiancé neglected her as well. Lack of support can cause a person so much pain that they succumb to suicide.

It was not just that her man was not around. She was predisposed to depression because of her childhood needs for attention. The lack of attention, understanding, and interaction contributed to her sadness and pain.

Learning to Swim

I almost drowned as a child. My mother would keep me away from water because of it. The pattern at swim training was to see full capacity. By the end of the training, the class was down to 3 people. People gave up.

Eventually, you will see the connections between your experience, your trauma responses, and your daily life, including anxieties and depression. In addition, you learn how to deal more sustainably with your triggers. Remember, when you know about yourself, people cannot play you.

I decided I wanted to learn to swim at the age of 25. Swimming was hard for me. It took me three years and multiple attempts in classes to learn to swim. Because I had the drowning experience, I had to overcome some things before taking to the learning. I was barred from the pool as a matter of protection. But that was avoiding the reality. Keeping me away from the lessons does not keep me from drowning. If I was on a boat and fell into the water, I would still drown because I did not learn how to swim. Learning how to swim is the solution, not avoiding water.

It is the same with your trauma. Avoiding your trauma is not going to keep you safe. You must move into the waters of your experience alongside a therapist that knows what he/she is doing. This support will make the difference. You will learn how to find your way in tumultuous situations and respond with healing to traumatic experiences.

My possibilities have expanded since working through my trauma. I told my mother that I wanted to be an actress when I was young. She called her godfather. He told her that it was a pipe dream. "She would need to know someone in Hollywood to be an actress. It is not going to happen." My mother got off the phone and told me to give up on my dream.

"He said it would not happen. Go and be a nurse or something." My family does not control my life and my future. I decided to put in the work. I moved to New York and became an actress. I have been in theatre and film. I was able to let go of the fear, insecurity, and negative energy that suggests that you stay in a lane that is lesser than your dreams. You do not need to become the best, brightest, and most celebrated in an area. That is motivated by wanting to show off or prove something to others. When you desire to do something for yourself, you will go after it regardless of the accolades. The more you work on your craft, the more clarity you will have.

If you write, for example, you may begin in one area. The universe will give you more clarity as you continue to write. You will discover more specifically what makes you happy or what areas you want to focus on. You will find inspiration in normal things and unusual places. You will dive into deep waters and swim. You don't have to be mainstream to be celebrated.

Resiliency in the Brain

Your brain will play tricks on you, telling you not to do the work in those areas of your healing. Your brain is lazy. It does not want to do the work. In your mind, the task is more difficult than it truly is. Once you begin doing it, you often find that it is less work and time than you thought.

When you begin in therapy and persist, you heal gradually. It will not be easy at first. You must focus on the progress to keep going back. If you look closely enough, the learning is there. You can apply what you learn to other areas of your life. The lessons will apply in your personal life, employment, and other areas. Therapy allows you to practice seeing things through another lens. You are better able to reframe your experience and persist.

It took me an abnormal amount of time to learn to swim, but I did not give up. I remember when I swam my first lap through the pool. I felt an immense sense of achievement. I was able to learn in a controlled environment with lifeguards on duty. I knew that if I was drowning, they would come to my rescue. I did not have a breakthrough in the first session of therapy. It took me weeks. I came back because I had not learned—I had not gotten the results of healing. It was important for me to go back to that supportive environment to get assistance in the healing journey. I persisted, and that is why I have made progress.

You will thank yourself as you persist. If you do not know how to do something, if you are not at the point of healing that allows you to manage your anxiety effectively, if you are hurting others out of your own sense of hurt, learn how to heal and do things differently. It is that simple. It is simple to decide to persist. The benefits, on the other side, are immense.

Many who are not choosing to persist are the biggest haters. You can be mad at the people who put in the work all you want. Your work ethic will speak for itself. Your healing will speak for itself. Authentic people are obvious in our society.

You are relearning the process to retrain your brain. The first step is to consider the options. You, like many, have a fear of the unknown. You can only rely on the perspectives and skills that you have. If you have not failed, you are not doing much. You may fail at times but consider all the other options. Connect with counselors that provide additional options—benefit from others' experience, especially professionals.

My switch was to become more open-minded. Things are not always black and white. Running from a situation is not the only answer. If you have a terrible boss, you could quit. You could also advocate for yourself. Speak up and tell your boss how you feel. If you are being used and abused, stand up for yourself. You have more options than your brain may have practiced. Lean into them. Persist with supportive and therapeutic environments and win. Healing is your reward.

Chapter 7: Prioritize You

Healthy Activities

Make time for what feeds you. We talk about this as self-care, but it is more of a mental health and well-being lifestyle. Awareness, perseverance, autonomy, and humility are habits more than just recreation.

Awareness. Generational trauma is not something you could control when you were a child. Your ancestors have experienced trauma as well. You live life with the historic trauma handed down to you. You cannot change that history, but you do have choices in the present to impact your future. You must become keenly aware of your opportunity to break cycles and change your future.

You must be able to acknowledge what you have done wrong. Your ancestors may have been the actors, but the choice is now up to you. You are responsible for making the changes and correct what is wrong. You must be aware that you are the decision-maker now. Inform your decisions with information. You have work to do in your life and community. Rather than seeing it as a race, the better model is community. Too often, we deflect and obscure the fact that our choices matter. You must take the responsibility to make the best choices for yourself and your community.

Perseverance. If you want to break the cycle of toxicity in your life and community, you must be the best version of yourself. You must heal your trauma. You must learn how to connect emotionally with authenticity. You must engage in a relationship with the intention to contribute health and wellness rather than to require someone to cater to you.

I remember seeing a show on MTV where a mother had several kids when she was younger and saddled the oldest child with the responsibility of taking care of the younger children. The mother rationalized that she must take the time now to experience life. She seemed unaware of the trauma she was inflicting on her daughter. She was ensuring that the generational trauma of a stolen childhood continues. She did not recognize the truth of perseverance—to identify your trauma, learn to address it, and practice healthier choice behavior.

Autonomy. You must ask how you will stop the cycle. You must not blame others for your choice set. No one needs to apologize before you begin to make better choices. Autonomy is not just about you doing what you want. It is about you making the best choices even if you must find new choices. You must be your best self. Connect with counseling. Read about healing and health. Identify what you can do and know that you can make a change. Your contribution to your generation will influence the next generation, their health and wellbeing.

Humility. Unlearn the toxic ways that you were raised. I hear adults say today, "My parents beat me because they cared." Not true. You are not supposed to be desensitized to abuse. Your parents beating the crap out of you is not discipline. Moreover, corporal punishment is not the only option for discipline. I hear people say, "If my mom and dad had not beat me, I would be dead in the streets right now." Not true.

You do not need to give in and perpetuate abusive behavior as a caring behavior. This is the same logical fallacy that supports your choice as an adult to stay in a toxic and abusive relationship. If abuse is caring, there is no need for change. Not true. All attention is not healthy attention. Seek healthy relationships based on personal responsibility and partnership. Escalation to anger and violence is not acceptable, normal, or healthy no matter how you were raised. Take some time and apply humility to realize that your training in trauma sets you up to seek the same reality with different faces. If you do not work on yourself, you will seek and support the same childhood experience as an adult.

Guilt Refusal

If you are not willing to conform or compromise to toxicity, people will attempt to make you feel guilty. People must respect your feelings, your choice, and your morals. If they can't, this is the beginning of a toxic relationship.

You may feel guilt, but often the culprits are the people around you that do not support your awareness, perseverance, autonomy, and humility. They make you feel bad about standing up for yourself. People want to make it seem like you have some responsibility for creating an environment where someone abuses, disrespects or bullies you. This is a logical fallacy with a traumatic effect when you set boundaries, especially the people who are now locked out, attempt to make you feel guilty for the access they are now denied.

I am not talking about guilt that makes you want to be a better person. If you know that you want to spend more time with your kids or nurture a significant relationship more, you will feel guilt. Lean into that. Refuse shame that creates triggers and poor choices. That is the negative to look out for. When guilt requires or metastasizes into shame, it is no longer useful.

I remember a writer/producer who was incredibly negative toward me. He triggered me in the context of perfection. He wanted me to be perfect, comparing me with my co-star. He limited my space and creativity. This abuse was considered normal.

I was a co-star in the production. I came into dress rehearsal frazzled because of the writer/producer's approach. My co-star commented negatively on my energy and asked if I wanted to talk about the feelings. "First of all, you are coming in with this energy. Do you want to talk about it?" I told her that I did not. She was offended. I apologized even though I was not wrong. She did not want to accept my apology.

The production team and actors convened for a huddle after our rehearsal. The writer/producer gave me a compliment saying that I will do great things. When the circle got around to the co-star, the situation went all the way left. She went on to throw me under the bus with the writer specifically saying that I spoke poorly about him. She blew it so out of proportion that the stage manager defended me and explained the inaccuracies of her rant. She continued.

The truth is that she often called me complaining about him. She informed me prior that the writer's method of operation was to put co-stars against each other. Ultimately, I completed the assignment. I showed up and was present even while they attempted to make me feel guilty about the whole situation. I knew that I was not the aggressor or the negative energy. I refused to accept the guilt, lean into my trigger, and lessen my craft in the face of their drama.

Finding You

I had to be okay with what my past was. I could not change the past. I needed to focus on my future. Now that you know how your past has influenced you, activate a level of consciousness. Time does not heal everything. Age does not bring wisdom. Effort heals and wisdom comes with learning and practice. Avoiding will not bring the growth and development that will support your success.

My priorities are better constructed because I know me and what I need to move forward. I reflect upon what I want for myself in the next 5 or 10 years. I am capable. Anything that seems impossible is impossible until it is done. No one can make me feel inferior or powerless. The challenge is to understand how to navigate through the challenges. If plan A does not work, move on to plan B. Refuse the inclination to attempt to fix plan A.

Exploration is an open book with no writing. Put in the work of the trial and error. It is not as defeating as toxicity. It is the ability to make mistakes and try again without judgement. Think about things that you loved. Revisit the reasons that you persisted or gave up. Live your life! People learn to put their lives on hold for multiple reasons. Those reasons often seem valid at the moment. Marriage, parenthood, career, caregiving for elderly parents, and many more decisions can result in delaying, limiting, or losing yourself altogether. It is not the loss that is lamentable. Find yourself again before you build faulty relationships, choices, and assumptions on your incomplete sense of self.

I met a woman that returned to ballet after her husband died. I met her doing background for a television show. She had the most amazing aura. She was in her 60s with silky gray hair when I met her. She also had a great pair of legs. I had to comment. "You have great legs. What is your secret?" She told me her story. I did not get all the details, but she put in the effort after her husband died and started dancing ballet in her 40s. She reflected upon what she wanted for her life. She searched for what was meaningful, how to make her life worthwhile.

Maybe it was a search for healing as well. She certainly found it. She danced ballet for 15 years by the time I met her. Did I mention that she had the best pair of legs?

She refused the normal excuses of "too late" and "too old." It is never too late for toxic people as well. It is never too late for you to prioritize yourself. The opportunity is to discover the authentic you after you put in the work of processing your trauma. Focus on internal advancement and seek clarity. Your progress is not measured in economic or career advancement. The measure of progress is your mental health, enhanced character, and beauty of spirit. This woman had an aura that made me feel at ease and happy in her presence. She evolved. That is the goal of prioritizing You.

Chapter 8: Take Care Body & Spirit

Too many people want to be caretakers without healing themselves. You cannot heal the world without healing yourself. If you don't work on yourself, you end up attempting to control people and deriving validation from that. You reinsure yourself with rejection when people refuse to accept your solutions. You must determine your challenges and triggers and create a lifestyle for addressing them. Seek health as a lifestyle after receiving therapy and prioritizing You.

Take Care

Inside and outside need to be taken care of. When you are in a good space emotionally, you attract positivity and opportunity. Become aware of the red flags in relationships. Protect your spirit and energy. Yet, the solution is not to live in a bubble. You must address the inclination to self-protect with a plan for health and safety beyond the bubble.

Let's talk about energy for a moment. The science about energy and vibration is well established. When a person has negative energy, it could seem like a dark cloud around them. When you engage with a person with negative energy, they drain your energy. You feel run-down and used up after spending time with them. You must make the decision not to engage with negative energy to the point where you are empty.

If you have lived in an area of low or toxic energy, you must get out of that situation. People will make you feel guilty about wanting something better for your life. As children, we are not able to move away and thrive. But as adults, we have choices. If your trauma includes a controlling person that oppresses or suffocates you, help may be needed to leave that scenario. Once again, therapy can help. If you feel empowered to make changes in your life, you only need to find different options and realize what is healthy for you.

The most important thing is to be in a healthy relationship. Refuse the inclination to rush into a situation that gets you out of your current situation but creates a worse situation. A friend of mine says, "Any relationship that begins fast and furious will end fast and furious." You have options and resources. You spend time on things that you want to do. Add healthy routines, better diet choices, and positive energy to your list of things you want to do.

You must go beyond the buzz words and fashionable statements. Research how new advancements neuropsychology can be applied to your healthy lifestyle choices. It is more than more money and more material things.

Meditation

My instructor was a classical pianist. When I told her about my process, she shared that she meditated. I ended up at her house learning how to meditate with a guru. The sensation calms my brain. It does not seem natural at first. I had to get to a place where I was not fighting to calm my brain. You often feel that you must do everything yourself and do everything on your ToDo List without hesitation and with ease. I am not sure what happened, but after 20 minutes of stillness, I was in a state of Zen. I found that stillness is critical. I never thought that I could calm myself down just by being still. In time, my spirit was sharpened. I was better able to pick up on energy, manage my energy, and move in positive energy spaces. I found a greater sense of being in tune with myself.

We often lead such busy lives that we do not comprehend what calm is. My experience is centered on perfection. As a girl growing up in a strict household, the pressure was to do things and do them right. It is not a complete statement to blame society for these pressures. You must decide what works for you and what does not. Once you get there, you will not give a damn about what the outside society wants. You will no longer need to fix everything. Situations are not the end of the world.

My spirit has become more sensitive. I am more aware. I can self-regulate. Even though I feel the energies in any room I enter, I can find peace in the experience. I am in a better space mentally and emotionally. Rather than freaking out and allowing anxiety to control you and send you to the sunken place, you can speak life, positivity and calm to your mind. Rather than sabotaging or setting yourself up, you quiet the negative thoughts and make decisions from a place of stillness.

The other critical element of meditation is to recognize the connections between your body, spirit, and behavior. As I became more in tune with my body, seeing my therapist, and addressing my responses to life's situations, I found a control that was based on balance rather than perfection. Through my work on myself, I no longer thought the situation was the cause of my anxiety. I blamed the moment as I puked my guts out when stressed. I had to tune in and understand the programming I received as a child. I was taught to worry and stress about perfection. With the work, I identified strategies that attended to my standards, protected my health, and provided me with a space for growth.

Accessing Law of Attraction

I saw the hurt in the world, but I realized that I did not have to associate myself with those people. I had to get in tune with the energy that I exude and the energy I attract. I choose to be around people that feed my positivity.

I write things down as a way of focusing my energy. I intentionally engage with the ideas in meditation, and that also leads to my daily life of attraction. I maintain the peace that is based on what I expect for my life. There is a reason why heart disease is the number one killer in the United States.

Often, the opportunities are in front of us, but we are not in the mental space to identify, access, and expand on them. The law of attraction says that you will attract what you focus on. For example, if I want to write a book, I have two choices positive and negative. I can focus on the negatives of lack of money, time, and expertise. Or, I can focus on the positives of accessing the money, time, and expertise.

The positive perspective will give us a positive outcome. You set yourself up to fail when you begin with a deficit mindset.

The frequency illusion is applicable here. This phenomenon is a simple construct that says you tend to see what you mentally fixate upon. You know this. If your friend gets a new red Volkswagen, you will see more red Volkswagens on the road. This is the frequency illusion.

Imagine if you focused on that thing you want to accomplish through meditation. Whatever you need to get it done will begin to come to you. You will notice the ingredients, tools, and mechanisms. It is not that people will necessarily walk up to you and help. But, as you get started, your momentum will push and pull you into situations where you have an opportunity.

Your mindset determines your success or failure. It is critical to feed your mind good stuff. Refuse to limit yourself. The bubble may seem safer. It is predictable. But you do not live with purpose in the bubble. You live ordinary and uninspired. Take care of your body and spirit and accomplish what you are born to do.

Chapter 9: Create the You Desired

The best way to contribute to society is to begin with yourself. I had to put in the work to create the me that I wanted. I had to stop the generational curse and refuse the toxicity in my life. Safety and security were incredibly important for me. I sought out help and found that safety and security start with me. I learned in therapy that life is a circle. You attract the familiar when you practice the mindset that was handed to you from your childhood. You attract safety and security when you practice a mindset of consideration and informed decision-making.

The awakening is powerful, but it does not happen naturally. It is worth it, but the cost is significant. Be brave enough to heal yourself and correct what began in your ancestors. Ask what you must do to ensure that your children do not experience the same trauma we experienced. It begins at home. I believe that better parents raise healthier children. Healthier children, biologically yours or otherwise, is the evidence of broken generational curses.

"Every woman who heals herself heals her children's children."
Liezel Graham

Conformity

People seem to want to be in groups and integrate with people toward conformity rather than risking uniqueness. You live in a new world. What worked 30 years ago does not work today. It may have never worked. You now have the opportunity to update your information and practices to what truly works. We too often defend toxic and abusive behavior as the norm or somehow acceptable as a tie to our past. Passively, we engage in childrearing practices like spanking because our parents did the same. Some parents take whipping to extremes beating children with cords and buckles. I know of instances where parents force their children to strip and enter the running shower to ensure the sting of the lash. This abuse is excused with references to fictitious situations that could have occurred if the child had not been beaten. We erroneously call this discipline as we cosign, saying, "I was beaten, and I turned out fine."

I beg to differ. You did not turn our fine if you sanction the abuse of another simply because you endured the same abuse. You ignore multiple studies that suggest that reading to a child, communicating effectively with children, and providing age-appropriate physical activities for children results in pro-social behavior, scholastic excellence, and mental health.

Some think they are woke because they resist new information and alternative ways of interacting with the world. But this is not woke or nonconformist. This is conformity to the status quo. You have been sold a bill of goods whenever you refuse to add additional insight to what you grew up understanding. Imagine a college professor who never reads or conducts research after graduating with a Ph.D. Imagine a surgeon who never updates her practice knowledge. Imagine an accountant who does not engage with new tax laws. You would not want either of them teaching you, performing your surgery, or handling your finances, respectively.

Being woke begins with You. Evaluate You first. Identify what your contribution is to the problem and solution. If you want to address racism, ask how to address it without being defeated. If you want to get to a place of better interactions among diverse people, you must begin with engaging people with greater grace, intention, and purpose. Blaming and pointing fingers, attempting to exact apologies will not result in your desired world. You must create a set of behaviors for yourself and share that mantra of behaviors with others.

Finding Your Tribe

Read. That is your first step. Get the information any way you can. Listen to podcasts, audiobooks, or YouTube videos. Just make sure that you feed your mind with information from multiple sources and from differing points of view. Identify a vision, purpose, and direction and go after it.

Reach out to communities that support, celebrate, and inspire you. I was able to find opportunities by joining Facebook groups. Groups have received some negative spin these days because many people engage groups to enhance the echo chamber of one-sided propaganda. More sustainably applied, groups are a way to ensure accountability, challenge, and question your point of view. You are not always right. You can take comfort in that fact. You can also take comfort in the fact that people exist as springboards, sounding boards, and speed bumps for your ideas.

When you find such a group, the still popular term is Tribe. Your tribe includes elements of following and leading. It is a group of mutual support and often collective activity. In your tribe, you experience the best of the phrase; two heads are better than one. You experience the power of community to make the impossible into I'M POSSIBLE.

Crabs in a Barrel of Pride

Many blame others for their problems. Others seek to fix things for someone else. I don't know if you are determined to be a perfectionist, a peacemaker, a martyr, a saint, or a sacrificial lamb, but I want you to find another role without your relationship to others. You feel responsible to the world, responsible for their thoughts about you because toxic people make you feel responsible. Toxic people made you feel like the problem is your fault, like you cannot make mistakes. You are not responsible for them, their thoughts, or their feelings. You are only responsible for yourself.

People often want to make noise and bully even in response to bullying. When the vulnerability, grace, and restorative justice of the process of healing comes up, many fall by the wayside. I have been focused on training my mind to finish what I start. I seek additional information. I find people who can help. I persevere through the work required. It seems like only the strong survive, but more specifically, the race is given to those that endure to the end. And pride must be set aside for healing to take place.

Pride is the final word here. Ask yourself what keeps you from seeking help and creating the You that you desire. Determine what hinders you from becoming the You that you deserve. I know the answer already. It is pride. Pride will keep you stuck. Pride will make you worry about what others will say if they find out that you received therapy. Pride will convince you that you don't have time, money, or attention span for your healing. Pride will tell you that one bad experience, one incompetent therapist, one missed appointment disqualifies the whole enterprise of help available to you. Resist pride and live.

Section III: Just for You

Chapter 10: You Are Not Alone

Death by Suicide and Silence

I remember a kid in college that died by suicide. He seemed so happy. I was surprised that he killed himself. He was a resident assistant like me. He was hugger, calm and collected. He was a nursing major. There were no signs visible that he was contemplating suicide. Only the Lord knows what he was feeling inside.

He could have felt that he had to be the man in every situation. He was Nigerian. He was always in a good mood. I knew him. He was reserved and respectful. His brother was the same way. He jumped out of a window—the worst way to go. He felt so alone and so much pain that he believed death was the only option.

The suicide occurred during the Summer. I found out through social media. It was a shock to everyone. All that knew him were in disbelief.

The dorms had large windows without fall barriers. He opened the window and leaned out. Three other friends were in the room. There were scaffolds outside the window, so those in the room did not think much of it. They thought he was looking for something. The friends were incredulous.

I have a Nigerian friend who explained the hesitation to seek counseling that is present in the culture. In addition, if someone dies by suicide, the family is shunned. The result is a group of people that do not seek help. Many communities are the same. We must normalize mental health and mental health services. This young man had the same opportunities as I had when he was in college. I went to a therapist when I found myself overwhelmed and frustrated. The community failed him by making him feel that he could not speak his truth.

One of my friends is a model. He sat for a shoot and posted the pictures in an art show. My friend posted it on his Instagram. Some family members from his home in Senegal called his parents and complained. They questioned whether he was gay because he was pictured with gold glitter on his body. His father demanded that the pictures be removed from Instagram because people were talking. I was flabbergasted and confused when I saw the post. Didn't they know about art? What does glitter have to do with being gay? It was closed-mindedness that is not good for the community and less good for an individual.

A life walking on eggshells worried about what people think and say about you is stressful. Instead, you must live with purpose. You must live to your full potential. You must not allow your community to tell you that you are terrible, unworthy, or not enough. Living your life to gain the praise and confirmation of a community garners you neither and leaves you miserable. Selfcare is physical, mental, emotional, and spiritual. If you feel that community standards limit you and stifle your growth, you must seek other foundations. Your voice is vital to the larger community of people who celebrate and inspire you. Speaking in your voice is critical to your holistic health and finding that tribe.

Dismissed in Community

People attempt to dismiss what my mother was and how it impacted me. I had to put a stop to the interactions that broke me and threaten to keep me down. People often say, "They did the best they could." I think the problem is that people, parents, believe that they know better. They feel that they have been through what the child is going through. They are so concerned about being right and in control that they make excuses for their actions. If they did it, it must be right. They are the parent.

The solution is to build a relationship with your children. Speaking poorly about your child to others should not be on the list. Children listen to what you say about them. Those messages stick to them. Parents shoulder a grand responsibility, but the way to execute that responsibility is not control. Parents can't be ready for every situation, but they can be prepared to handle them.

I remember working at a New Year's Eve event in time square. A mother and daughter were kicked out because they were fist fighting. I did not blame the child. I blamed the mother. I could not understand how you raise a child that you feel comfortable fist fighting. You failed if that is your family dynamic. The parent-child dynamic should not be dictator to peasant. Parents will not do everything correctly, but when they recognize their error, an apology is warranted. The apology teaches emotional communication—the precursor to empathy. Next, explain the process and how you made the decision even though it was wrong. The explanation teaches decision-making. Refuse closed-mindedness. That is not wise or a way to develop wisdom in a child.

I want you to know that you are not alone. People would tell me, "That's your mom. She will always be your mom." Don't allow people to make you think that pain, abuse, and trauma is acceptable, even excusable after the fact when you are an adult. Life should not be that way. As I grew and became more aware of the toxicity, I had to limit my exposure to my mother.

The solution is not a one-size-fits-all. I do not suggest that all children limit their contact with their parents even when they are toxic. If you can repair the relationship through discussions or counseling with a third party, take that step. Consider options for repairing the relationship, but do not dismiss the need to correct behavior. If the parent refuses to admit and change their behavior, that choice is a choice to limit contact. You must refuse toxicity in your life if you are going to thrive. It is more toxic when toxicity comes from a family member. It is dangerously toxic when toxicity comes from a parent.

Speak Your Truth

I still wake up angry sometimes because my mother does not understand where I am coming from. That is with limiting my exposure to her. Energy does not lie. Energy also is not created or destroyed. It is only changed for purpose. Toxicity will change your energy into despair. Your intentional positivity will turn your energy into passion. You playing small does not help society, as Williamson famously wrote.

You will have flash-backs and experience triggers. The experiences stay with you even in your healing. My triggers, like others, come from my traumas. Often, helplessness is the feeling. I have a voice. I am strong. I am capable regardless of what people think of me. I refuse to allow my trauma to limit or silence me.

Rather than running away from your trauma, you must work through it. Rather than being bullied by that feeling, you must stand up and address them. Sometimes, you need help to create these strategies. Accept that help. Recognize. Heal. Prosper. That is my process. Take your power back and thrive. Those traumas that you do not address will act as weights limiting your momentum. They act as silencers choking out your voice.

Your work will not be done because you worked through one situation. Keep the option open to return to therapy after you have overcome any one issue. Different life situations, new experiences and relationships may remind you of trauma or trigger you. If your strategies don't work for this new trigger, work to develop new ones. There is no place for shame. Get the help you need.

Also, I want you to keep the community and the individual separate. Trends, community, and movements are useful to the process in the community. If you are in a relationship, working with the person is critical and definitional. Refuse the toxicity of movements that speak ill of one part of the partnership. For example, I talked with a woman that was having a disagreement with her husband. Rather than discussing the disagreement, she launched into a diatribe about the superiority of women, feminism, and girl power. I disagreed. The solution to her disagreement with her husband was not found in a movement. The solution is a one-to-one authentic, honest, and open discussion. I did not allow her to coop a movement to get out of healthy communication with her husband.

I use my voice, speak up, and assert my autonomy. I became fearless to stand confident in my space. If you are like most of us, you do not realize how strong you are. You may be afraid of failure or of what people may think. You will not know what is possible unless you step out and speak up. Your voice requires bravery. Fear is immaterial always, especially when your pain, trauma, and grief suggest that suicide is a viable option. When suicide is on the table, all other options are possible. I would rather you stand in the face of cultural, community and parental defiance rather than succumb to suicidal ideation. The height of toxicity is to believe that silencing your truth is better than contradicting your community.

You are not required to sit and accept whatever comes to you without speaking up. Many believe what you believe but are not brave enough to speak up. The world will not be a better place unless we strive to be better people. You must hold yourself accountable for what is required to make those "better" changes. You must foster authenticity, honesty, and open discussion. If you encounter people who are uncomfortable with that, continue to speak your truth. Leave them alone if they refuse to participate constructively.

Chapter 11: No Longer Bound

Out of Control

I have noticed that many approach life as a "get them before they get me" transaction. Take note of the signs. If you feel uncomfortable, you must speak up and find ways to move to another option.

Understand that everyone is different. Everyone has a different story. Everything is not black and white. Change is good. Often, change is required. Life is unpredictable. Trying to control everything around you will exhaust you. The need is security. You want to feel safe. When I found myself prioritizing that above all, I stopped. Learning is not always safe.

I work with kids. Some of my colleagues and parents think that one size will fit all. It does not. Many kids move to advanced grades without the knowledge they need to succeed. I recommend that parents stay involved with their children's education. Not just awareness and observation, but also engage in the child's passions. Connect their passion to their learning.

I was raised to think that children were supposed to be obedient and quiet. I was punished a lot because I was hyperactive and curious. That foundation was broken as I got older because the lessons of obedience and silence failed me. I was not happy being that way. My basic needs were not met. I realized that I needed help to break down the training I received as a child and retrain myself to make mistakes without feeling that it was the end of the world. That perfectionism supported insecurity and a search for validation. More tragic, it mutes your feelings and limits your inner voice, reflectiveness, and emotional health. You tend to put your emotions last and put others before yourself. You miss the opportunities to discover the different layers of yourself. You miss the chance to see that you are enough and growing.

Once is Enough

I do not allow people to mistreat me more than once. I have not felt like other bosses have been abusive since my first experience. My intentional setting of boundaries made the difference. The freedom you internalize by giving yourself the out is amazing. You are not required to stay in any situation that is abusive and unhealthy.

You may feel guilty because you automatically assume that situations are your fault and that you are the problem. That is what abusers teach. They attempt to convince you that you caused them to get mad and hit or otherwise abuse you. If you are with someone who makes you feel judged, flawed, and unworthy, you must get away from that person. Relationships should make you feel empowered. There are compromises, but they are always based on support, mutual respect, reciprocity, and collaborative development. They are healthiest when each person has come to the relationship after their personal development. Establish your security, happiness, and health prior to the relationship. Do not seek those through the relationship. That is an unfair and erroneous expectation.

Boundaries are critical in every relationship. You must know how you want to be treated and know how to assess and treat others the way they want to be treated. That is a vital initial conversation. The relationship develops as you experience situations where you have the opportunity to speak up and express how their actions make you feel. If a change needs to be made, the decision is to either accept or go your separate ways.

The most insidious example is one where someone does not know how to disagree appropriately. You must set the agreements, the boundaries, early in the relationship. If you have someone who calls you out of your name when they get angry or disagree, and that is against your established boundaries, the relationship will fail eventually. Failure to uphold your boundaries instills resentment. Resentment will cause relationship stress. Stress is not the healthy position of any relationship.

The critical skill is that of expression. I was never trained growing up to express myself. I was an outspoken person, but I did not understand the hurt and the process within my body. The self-awareness and the ability to know myself without feeling judged and ashamed was a part of my healing process. Healing empowered me and caused a desire to advocate and train people to develop their voice. Life should not be about hurt, pain, and repeated poor relationships. If you go through the healing process, you will find that you have been holding yourself back. Your future is what you make it. No one can keep you bound.

Serenity rather than Control

Serenity is the name, but gaining it is a balance between asserting yourself and trusting the law of attraction or other universal laws. Serenity is not about avoiding the issue. Conflict is an opportunity for resolution. Resolution requires conflict when two or more parties disagree. You must decide whether something is important enough to address. You must also address it head-on, not passively. Passive aggressive energy is not trusting energy. People who choose passive aggressiveness have not learned to express themselves or fear that their expression will result in conflict; it may. But the end of that is a lesson. You learn about your expression, the person's capacity for resolution, and maybe techniques for your next conflict encounter.

Serenity provides a foundation of inner peace, whereas control creates stress. Attempting to control situations and people will lead to exhaustion. You will trigger your insecurities from the past and risk lashing out in the situation. The worst outcome is that you may lash out without a perspective on the current challenge. You may speak and act in reaction to your prior experience leaving the current person clueless about where the reaction is coming from.

Consider that you are in control as you are able to display patience while making your intentions known and managing your energy. When you get to a place of serenity, it changes your perspective on life. You will encounter bad people. You are not required to stay in their presence. This is enforcing your boundaries.

You must be ready. An open mind and learning from other people's stories is a valuable start. You will learn when you listen to the stories of others. The things that you are avoiding are the things that can control you. They can sneak up and trigger reactions in you. Serenity is about working through your past, acknowledging it, and choosing to move forward intentionally. Often, you will need help. Seek that help. Persist in getting that help.

Serenity will require a leap of faith, resulting in your mindset shift. The switch will not happen overnight. You will not find success, riches, and fame as a solution. People think that self-care is about pampering and a moment of comfort. It is an ongoing, daily practice. Unpredictable things will occur. In those situations, your self-care is applied. Healing is the ability to choose serenity rather than control. To engage in the daily realities of the world, accepting the things that you cannot change. Also, by setting boundaries, choosing serenity, you can speak up for yourself when needed and walk away when appropriate.

My ending is nowhere near because my story has yet to be told. I may be a disappointment to some, but I am an inspiration to many. It is time to discover your layers. Take the time to discover. You will always be a human with challenges. Your situation will not be perfect. Life is about reflection and growth. Seek to improve yourself.

Toxic environments and relationships can become comfortable. But listen to the feelings of discomfort—those moments that are breaking points for you. This is God signaling you that there is a bigger world out there. If you feel that the devil you do not know is more dangerous, switch your mindset to understand that devils are not the only option. Consider that situations are not to last always. Get in. Learn the lesson and be willing to move on.

I wrote a quote on my Instagram page based on a situation I had to walk away from:

The discomfort and anxiety you feel in certain situations is your purpose, signaling you that there is more in store for you. Move on and move up.

Chapter 12: Living Through Trauma

Resiliency in Action

Our bodies relate to our brain, whether we intentionally manage it or not. Your body will hold the experiences of trauma and express it in the form of sickness. Healing is recognizing the responses of the body where emotions express themselves physically.

Resilience is simply not giving up. It is making it through the difficult times. Challenges will come. You face them and gain wisdom from them. You must ask yourself how these experiences apply to your future. This process builds your character and makes you a better person. Some people think that the experience makes you better. People attempt to control you or explain their failures as good for you. Yet, the experience is not the determinant of your character development. The determinant is how you respond to each situation.

Your personal life is yours to reveal. A critical lesson in life and resilience is to share yourself only with people who are concerned, capable, and consistent with compassion. Healthy relationships will not remind you of your trauma. They will not have the same pattern of the experiences and interactions that broke you.

I remember an ex-boyfriend who often said, "I know you." He thought he knew me better than I knew myself. I thought it was a good thing that he wanted to know me. I soon found out that my past was used when we had disagreements. He knew some facts, but he did not care about my evolution. He was not capable of holding my vulnerability with compassion. He was not consistent with the nurture and respect I needed to continue my growth.

One thing that I noticed in negative relationships is a tendency to point out your flaws. I was always labeled as the "bad kid" as a child because I wanted to have fun, touch things, and experience life. When negative relations are not able to get their way, they become abusive. I saw that pattern early with my mother.

You must distinguish between healthy relationships and unhealthy relationships. I remember moments when I was triggered to relive experiences from my past. Those were moments when I was vulnerable. Those moments tell you something that you must listen to. Unhealthy relationships will always offer their reflection and their reasons that you should continue with them in the same vulnerability. They require more from you than they are willing to contribute. They use your vulnerability against you. They will attempt to make you think that your vulnerability is a flaw in your character. Notice this perspective and pattern. Without noticing, you get to a point where you are concerned about their anger, disappointment, and other emotions more than your safety, security, and health.

I am definitely a work in progress. Early on in relationships, I take the stance that "nobody is perfect" because I am not perfect. This is a truth that you must clarify in your experience. You will see flags in relationships early on. Listen, observe, and make decisions based on a sober view of what you see.

Nobody is perfect, but you must take care especially based on your past. If you grew up in an abusive relationship fueled by alcohol, it is not a "nobody's perfect" moment when you encounter a relationship that has features of an abusive relationship fueled by alcohol. No matter how the person is dressed up and presents themselves, the determinant is you, not them. I knew all the flags of that experience. I thought that he could change. I was still gullible in that situation, wanting to give the benefit of the doubt.

DO NOT REPEAT THE PATTERN IN ADULT RELATIONSHIPS THAT BROKE YOU AS A CHILD.

Anxiety

When you feel anxiety, your task is to find healing instead. Trauma leaves you broken, but you can heal. You have an experience that contributes to brokenness. You have a weight on your shoulders that weigh you down.

Often, anxiety manifests as a feeling that someone is standing in your way, judging you swiftly, harshly, and without mercy. Sometimes, you do have people who stand between you and your goals. Some people ask, "Who do you think you are? What makes you think that you can succeed?" Those statements can also be internalized, and subconsciously, you repeat them in your mind.

I remember a co-worker that quit a job the same week she was hired. She told me about how her health suffered during that period. She also told me about her home life and the fact that she was her sole support. She went through a 3-month process to get the job. She was not aware of the strategy, the promise, or the plan in her life for the job. She gave up on the job, but she also gave up on herself. She could not allow herself to make mistakes in that first week.

You must not allow your anxiety to get the best of you every time. My approach is to refocus my mind on the causes of my anxiety, the steps of the process before me, and the outcomes that result from my perseverance.

Be honest with your origin story. Your childhood is often where the patterns are constructed. Your inner voice is trained there. Begin to deconstruct what you were taught. Again, filter through concern, capability, and consistency of compassion rather than only evaluating based on your experience.

Review the steps of the task at hand. Get help if needed. Ask questions. Write and rewrite if needed to ensure both your comprehension and comfort with the steps. Move toward a point where you can follow the steps like instructions. If you begin with step one, you are assured of reaching to completion of the task.

Envision the outcomes that result from your effort and perseverance. It may seem simple or rudimentary (maybe even silly), but sit intentionally to meditate on a vision of completion and the peace, opportunity, and progress that results. Many authors have demonstrated the power of vision to encourage achievement. From professional athletes to corporate salespersons, several industries promote mindfulness to reduce anxiety, encourage progress, and increase productivity.

Addressing Anxiety and Trauma

You must adopt a strategy, promise, and plan to persist. When you stick with it and work through it, you gain experience. The wisdom comes from processing those lessons. Processing means that you break down what you learned and attempt to apply it in other areas, and you note the outcomes compared to your desires.

I don't know if that employee knew or cared about her 401k, but employers do not give it to you until after a probationary period. They do that because people do not persist. She did not, and she gave up on a benefit. I am sure she felt like it was her against all others. I am certain that she did not reach out for help. I do not know if it was trauma or anxiety that kept her from persisting. I only know that she did not.

You do not have to feel like it is you against the world with your back against the wall. You can address the trauma. You can manage the anxiety. Keep setting appropriate boundaries that support healthy relationships. Keep prioritizing yourself, securing your health and happiness. Continue seeking help and finding a supportive community. Persist in your self-care ritual learning, creating, and growing. Never stop creating your Best Self. The world will be better because of your persistence.

www.ingramcontent.com/pod-product-compliance
Lightning Source LLC
LaVergne TN
LVHW051702080426
835511LV00017B/2683